ESTHER

CHARACTER UNDER PRESSURE

PATTY
PELL

9 STUDIES
FOR INDIVIDUALS
OR GROUPS

Life
Builder
Study

INTER-VARSITY PRESS
36 Causton Street, London SW1P 4ST, England
Email: ivp@ivpbooks.com
Website: www.ivpbooks.com

*Originally published in the United States of America in the LifeGuide® Bible Studies series
in 1995 by InterVarsity Press, Downers Grove, Illinois
Second edition published 2002
First published in Great Britain by Scripture Union in 2004
This edition published in Great Britain by Inter-Varsity Press 2018*

British Library Cataloguing-in-Publication Data
A catalogue record for this book is available from the British Library.

ISBN: 978–1–78359–786–4

*Inter-Varsity Press publishes Christian books that are true to the Bible and that communicate
the gospel, develop discipleship and strengthen the church for its mission in the world.*

*IVP originated within the Inter-Varsity Fellowship, now the Universities and Colleges Christian
Fellowship, a student movement connecting Christian Unions in universities and colleges
throughout Great Britain, and a member movement of the International Fellowship of Evangelical
Students. Website: www.uccf.org.uk. That historic association is maintained, and all senior IVP
staff and committee members subscribe to the UCCF Basis of Faith.*

Contents

GETTING THE MOST OUT OF *ESTHER* ——————————— 5

1 Esther 1   **A Little Respect** ——————— 9

2 Esther 2   **Trusting God's Work** ———————13

3 Esther 3   **Evaluating Advice** ———————18

4 Esther 4   **Doing the Right Thing** ———————22

5 Esther 5   **The Heart of the Matter** ————26

6 Esther 6   **Recognizing Unrighteousness** ——30

7 Esther 7   **Character No Matter What** ———34

8 Esther 8   **Praising God's Faithfulness** ———38

9 Esther 9—10   **Remembering & Celebrating** ——42

Leader's Notes —————————————————47

Getting the Most Out of *Esther*

"Just Do It" has been a successful and popular slogan for the athletic company Nike. It refers to getting in shape and participating no matter what the physical or mental strain. But the slogan brings something else to my mind after spending time in the book of Esther: it reminds me to *just do it*—do the right thing no matter what the consequences.

In the book of Esther we see the lives of several characters played out. There are those people who are selfish and prideful, seeking only personal recognition, and there are those who risk everything for others and choose integrity in the face of great opposition. Esther is a book about developing godly character. In the midst of a culture that does not emphasize doing what is right, this book speaks to us in profound ways.

As we read through the events of Esther, we are given a description of what godly character is and what it is not. But there is another very strong theme that weaves in and around the theme of character: God is working in the circumstances and events of people's lives to bring about his plans. God is the director, the conductor, the weaver. As God works in our lives, we must choose what is right so that we can be a part of God's plan.

The events of this powerful book take place in Persia during the reign of King Xerxes from 486 to 465 B.C. It has been over one hundred years since the beginning of the exile, and some Jews have returned to Jerusalem. The story is set in the city of Susa, which is where the king has his winter palace. It involves the whole of the Jewish people but revolves around the lives of

King Xerxes, Esther, her uncle Mordecai and Haman, the king's highest noble.

Esther's story presents the last major threat to the Jewish people in the Old Testament period. The threat and the Jews' deliverance are recorded in this book. The Jewish festival of Purim, which is still celebrated today, is established in Esther, which accounts for the book's great popularity among the Jewish people. It is a wonderful story of God's providence and the character of his people told with humor, irony, repetition and contrast. The book of Esther certainly proclaims faith in God's protection of his people.

Esther will stir us to examine our character, the deep aspects of our hearts. It will encourage us in taking a stand for what is right and give us courage that God is still in control. It is a book that we need to study so that we can glorify God with our whole being and begin to be witnesses in our world because of our integrity. If we allow the themes of Esther to penetrate our lives, we will begin to stop and question our actions and thoughts, and align them with God's desire.

May your study in Esther produce in you a longing for consistent godly character.

Suggestions for Individual Study

1. As you begin each study, pray that God will speak to you through his Word.

2. Read the introduction to the study and respond to the personal reflection question or exercise. This is designed to help you focus on God and on the theme of the study.

3. Each study deals with a particular passage—so that you can delve into the author's meaning in that context. Read and reread the passage to be studied. If you are studying a book, it will be helpful to read through the entire book prior to the first study. The questions are written using the language of the New

International Version, so you may wish to use that version of the Bible. The New Revised Standard Version is also recommended.

4. This is an inductive Bible study, designed to help you discover for yourself what Scripture is saying. The study includes three types of questions. *Observation* questions ask about the basic facts: who, what, when, where and how. *Interpretation* questions delve into the meaning of the passage. *Application* questions help you discover the implications of the text for growing in Christ. These three keys unlock the treasures of Scripture.

Write your answers to the questions in the spaces provided or in a personal journal. Writing can bring clarity and deeper understanding of yourself and of God's Word.

5. It might be good to have a Bible dictionary handy. Use it to look up any unfamiliar words, names or places.

6. Use the prayer suggestion to guide you in thanking God for what you have learned and to pray about the applications that have come to mind.

7. You may want to go on to the suggestion under "Now or Later," or you may want to use that idea for your next study.

Suggestions for Members of a Group Study

1. Come to the study prepared. Follow the suggestions for individual study mentioned above. You will find that careful preparation will greatly enrich your time spent in group discussion.

2. Be willing to participate in the discussion. The leader of your group will not be lecturing. Instead, he or she will be encouraging the members of the group to discuss what they have learned. The leader will be asking the questions that are found in this guide.

3. Stick to the topic being discussed. Your answers should be based on the verses which are the focus of the discussion and not on outside authorities such as commentaries or speakers. These studies focus on a particular passage of Scripture. Only rarely should you refer to other portions of the Bible. This allows for everyone to participate in in-depth study on equal ground.

4. Be sensitive to the other members of the group. Listen attentively when they describe what they have learned. You may be surprised by their insights! Each question assumes a variety of answers. Many questions do not have "right" answers, particularly questions that aim at meaning or application. Instead the questions push us to explore the passage more thoroughly.

When possible, link what you say to the comments of others. Also, be affirming whenever you can. This will encourage some of the more hesitant members of the group to participate.

5. Be careful not to dominate the discussion. We are sometimes so eager to express our thoughts that we leave too little opportunity for others to respond. By all means participate! But allow others to also.

6. Expect God to teach you through the passage being discussed and through the other members of the group. Pray that you will have an enjoyable and profitable time together, but also that as a result of the study you will find ways that you can take action individually and/or as a group.

7. Remember that anything said in the group is considered confidential and should not be discussed outside the group unless specific permission is given to do so.

8. If you are the group leader, you will find additional suggestions at the back of the guide.

1

A Little Respect

One of my favorite and most influential teachers was a high school English teacher. His class was extremely difficult and challenging, but I loved it and worked diligently in order to do well. The reason I respected this teacher so much is that he listened to me and valued me.

We would all like to be respected by others, so we try many ways of gaining that respect. Some try to gain it through controlling others or by demanding it. However, one of the ways respect is gained is by appreciating others and showing them respect.

GROUP DISCUSSION. Think of one person you respect. Describe some characteristics of this person and what he or she did to gain your respect.

PERSONAL REFLECTION. What are some characteristics in your life for which your friends might respect you? disrespect you?

King Xerxes made a habit of throwing lavish parties and celebrations. This particular celebration sets the scene for many of
the events in book of Esther: conflict, plots and schemes, brav-
ery, and deliverance. *Read Esther 1.*

1. Try to imagine yourself at this banquet. What would you be
experiencing (sights, sounds, smells and so on)?

2. Describe the various people we encounter in this chapter.

3. Why might the king have given such an extravagant party
(vv. 2-8)?

4. What might be the reason King Xerxes asks Queen Vashti to
come to him (vv. 10-11)?

5. The king's request places Vashti in a difficult position. What factors would she have been weighing in her decision (v. 12)?

6. What can we observe about King Xerxes' character so far?

7. Think of a time when you were asked to do something you were uncomfortable doing. How did you feel?

8. Why did the wise men perceive Queen Vashti's refusal to be dangerous to the kingdom (vv. 16-20)?

9. How does each of the main characters in this chapter (King Xerxes, Vashti, the wise men) view gaining and maintaining respect?

10. How does respect actually develop between people?

---

11. What are some ways you have been trying to gain respect that are not godly or helpful?

---

12. Describe one thing that you can do this week to show someone respect.

Thank God for those in your life who you respect, or pray that God will help you show respect to those around you.

Now or Later

Journal about some of the times you have disrespected people in your life. Pray through each of those experiences, asking God for forgiveness. If needed, write a note to those people asking for forgiveness.

2

Trusting God's Work

When the curtain rises and the play begins, we see and hear the actors and actresses tell a story. But the most important person in the play is not on the stage. The director is the one who has instructed the cast for months on where to stand and sit, and when and how to say a line. The director is behind the scenes giving final instructions, touching up makeup and encouraging the players. The play is a success because of the director, who has orchestrated every detail of the play.

In the book of Esther, God is not mentioned, but he is the key figure in the story. He works through the circumstances to place everything in order so that his plans will be accomplished. God is the director of our lives as well. As we look back at different times in our lives, we can see his handprints all over. Our response to him is to look for his hand moving and to trust his direction.

GROUP DISCUSSION. Describe a time in your past when you saw

God work through circumstances in your life to bring something about.

PERSONAL REFLECTION. Journal about how God has used circumstances to prepare you for your current role in God's work in the world.

The plan that is put into action to replace Queen Vashti is extensive and detailed. It takes approximately four years to complete. *Read Esther 2.*

1. Summarize the plan to find a new queen that King Xerxes put into action (vv. 1-4).

2. How does Esther enter the story and become the queen (vv. 5-17)?

3. Put yourself in the shoes of either Esther or Mordecai. How

would each of these characters have felt throughout this process?

---

4. The author mentions three times that Esther won approval in someone's eyes (vv. 9, 15, 17). What does this tell us about Esther?

---

5. Think of someone you know who finds favor with others because of their presence and personality. How can you begin living out one of the characteristics of this person in your own life?

---

6. Many young women were brought to the palace and placed in the harem. What was the role of these women, and how would Esther's life, role and rights be different from the harem when she became queen?

7. The author mentions several times that Mordecai instructed Esther to keep her identity hidden. What might have motivated that request?

8. How does Mordecai enter into the plot of the story (vv. 19-23)?

9. What does this glimpse of Mordecai's life tell us about his character?

10. Even though God has not been directly mentioned in the book, where do you see his hand moving in the story so far?

11. Where do you see God's hand moving in circumstances in your life right now?

How do you think he wants you to respond?

Pray for the ability to see God's hand working in your circumstances whether they are currently positive or negative.

Now or Later

Choose another biblical figure like Moses or David. Look through the story of their lives to see how God used circumstances to prepare them for their role in God's work.

3

Evaluating Advice

No one has "any right to counsel others who is not ready to hear and follow the counsel of the Lord." This quote from A. W. Tozer reminds me of the responsibility we have in giving advice to others. It is a serious thing to give counsel, and it is also a serious step to take the counsel of our friends. So often we give quick advice to one another without truly understanding the situation or without pure motives. Part of godly character is knowing how to evaluate the advice we receive and in turn to offer sound and wise counsel without looking to benefit ourselves.

GROUP DISCUSSION. Together make a list of people and sources from which we can take advice. Then evaluate the positives and negatives of each item on the list.

PERSONAL REFLECTION. List all the factors you use to evaluate someone's advice. What do you look for, think about, disregard and so on?

The events of this chapter would be frightening to read as a Jewish person. They describe the hostility in the world that was directed toward the Jewish people. *Read Esther 3.*

---

1. List all the words and phrases in this chapter that bring to mind tragedy or conflict.

---

2. What is the conflict between Haman and Mordecai that causes Haman's intense reaction to Mordecai (vv. 2-6)?

What does it feel like to be in this kind of conflict situation?

---

3. Describe the atmosphere of the kingdom after the edict had been proclaimed.

---

4. How does Haman persuade the king to adopt his plan to destroy the Jews (vv. 8-9)?

5. Think of a time in your life when you have been tempted to use half-truths and lies to convince someone. What were your thoughts and feelings at the time?

6. Describe the orders contained in the king's edict (v. 13).

7. In verses 12-14 the words *each, every* and *all* are repeated frequently. What might the author have been trying to communicate in this detailed description of the edict?

8. What have we learned about Haman's character in this chapter?

9. This chapter gives us even more detail about who King Xerxes was. What do we learn about him?

10. How might our character be reflected in the way we give or receive advice?

---

11. How might you guard against giving unwise advice?

---

12. What are some ways you can evaluate the advice you receive from others?

Pray for the people in your life who seek your counsel. Pray for your advice to be godly and sound.

Now or Later
Think through a current situation where you are either being asked for your advice or are seeking counsel. How has this study changed the way you will approach that situation?

4

Doing the
Right Thing

Laszlo Tokes was a pastor in Timisoara, Romania, during the reign of Ceausescu under the communist regime. Tokes had dedicated his life to bringing about revival in the church in Romania despite opposition and danger. He risked his life to preach the gospel and stand up against the communist government. Because of his courage and integrity he helped the people to win their freedom.

God places us in situations where he wants to use us, and in those situations we are faced with the choice of doing what God calls us to do or doing what is against God. We may never face circumstances like those of Laszlo Tokes, but doing what is right includes everything from giving back extra change when a cashier makes a mistake to standing up for justice in a dangerous situation. Whether the stakes are large or small, it takes the same character qualities of courage and moral strength to choose what is right.

GROUP DISCUSSION. As a group, find and cut out articles in the newspaper or in magazines about people's choices in difficult situations. Have the group choose one or two of the best illustrations, and discuss what would be the right thing to do in that situation. Talk through the complexity of the situation and what the consequences might have been if a different choice had been made.

PERSONAL REFLECTION. Reflect on an instance in your life where obeying God's call meant taking a risk or facing difficult consequences.

This chapter is the pivotal section of Esther's story. Her character is clearly demonstrated in her responses and choices in this chapter. *Read Esther 4.*

---

1. What is the sequence of events?

---

2. What does the response of Mordecai and the Jews to Haman's plot tell us about the Jews in Persia at that time?

---

3. How does the fasting of the Jewish people in verse 3 contrast with parts of the first three chapters?

4. What is the progression of responses that we see in Esther?

5. What do you think Esther may have been feeling at different points in her responses (vv. 9-11)?

6. Think of a situation God called you to in which obeying meant facing great risks. What was your first reaction, and what were your feelings when God called you?

7. What was Mordecai's perspective of Esther's role and responsibility in the situation?

8. How do Mordecai's arguments in verses 12-14 persuade Esther to go to the king?

9. In this chapter, how do we see God's sovereignty and people's responses working together?

_____

10. What character qualities does Esther show throughout this passage?

_____

11. Think of a present context in which you think God may have placed you to do his will. What risks do you face in doing the right thing in this situation?

What character qualities must you exhibit in order to do the right thing?

Ask God for the courage to be obedient in the current circumstances in your life.

Now or Later

Rent a movie such as *Remember the Titans* or *It Could Happen to You,* and discuss the themes from this chapter that you see in the movie. Identify the themes you see being embraced and the characteristics that are not shown.

5

The Heart
of the Matter

My schoolteacher husband came home from work one day with an unpleasant note from a parent. The note expressed anger and concern over his performance as a teacher. Scott was very wounded and puzzled by the note, but he made an appointment to meet with the parent the next day. In the face of a situation that could have led to bitterness and anger, I watched him respond with courage, compassion and humility. Because of his response, the misunderstanding was clarified and the relationship was reconciled.

Our response to difficult tasks or people that anger us tells a great deal about our character. Do we face these situations with courage and humility or with anger, bitterness and pride?

GROUP DISCUSSION. Divide into pairs within the group. Pretend that one of you is a newspaper reporter who has the opportunity to interview Esther about the events of chapters 1—4. The other person is Esther. Spend several minutes interviewing

Esther as she prepares to approach the king. Then discuss what the group discovers through the mock interviews.

PERSONAL REFLECTION. Identify a recent time where you responded to a situation with anger or bitterness. Think through the reasons you responded that way and how you felt during and after the experience.

Esther and Haman are a lesson in contrasts throughout the book. In this study we will see the vast differences between what is inside Esther and Haman. *Read Esther 5.*

---

1. What risks does Esther take in verses 1-8?

---

2. Put yourself in Esther's shoes at this point in the story. What would she be feeling and thinking?

---

3. Look back at 4:15-16. What enabled Esther to face the risk of going to the king without being summoned?

4. How can the support of other believers be helpful to you in the midst of a trial you are going through now?

What makes it difficult at times to ask for help and support?

---

5. Esther asks the king and Haman to attend a banquet. What may have been the reason for such a request (vv. 4-8)?

---

6. What do we learn about Haman's character in verses 9-14?

---

7. If you were a newspaper interviewer talking with Haman at this point, what questions would you ask him?

How might Haman respond to these questions?

8. How does the passage contrast Esther's and Haman's character?

9. Where in your own life do you see the qualities of Esther and the qualities of Haman?

10. In what current situation can you try to respond with the courage and humility of Esther?

Pray for courage and humility in responding to specific people and situations in your life currently.

Now or Later

Haman was consumed with Mordecai even though he had so many other things: wealth, prestige, sons and recognition. His feelings toward Mordecai soured the good things Haman had in life.

There may be one thing in our lives that consumes us to the detriment of all the other blessings God has given us. Take a step of courage to journal, pray or talk with a friend about what might be consuming in your life. Once you identify it, be sure to enter into God's presence and pray for the ability to address the issue in a healthy and godly way.

6

Recognizing Unrighteousness

When I take an honest look at myself, I see many ugly spots that mar my character. One of my ugliest traits is my desire to make myself look better than others. This ungodly character trait seeps into my relationships and damages intimacy.

For each of us there are things about our character that are displeasing to God; perhaps it is pride or arrogance, selfish ambition or manipulation. Because we let those things grow in our lives rather than allowing God to remove them, we experience various consequences of our unrighteousness.

GROUP DISCUSSION. Hand out a piece of paper to each member of the group. Have each person answer the following question and then depict the answer in some creative fashion, such as drawing a picture, writing a short poem, writing words in certain patterns and so on: What is one aspect of your character you would like to be more Christlike?

PERSONAL REFLECTION. Make a list of all the Christlike qualities that come to mind. Pray through this list in regard to your own life. Let the Holy Spirit guide your prayers and speak to you along the way. Be open to discovering a quality you need to work on in yourself.

Haman's experience in this chapter is exactly what Jesus describes centuries later as he reclines in the home of a prominent Pharisee. "For everyone who exalts himself will be humbled, and he who humbles himself will be exalted" (Luke 14:11). *Read Esther 6.*

---

1. What events in this chapter seem coincidental but lead to the development of the story?

---

2. How does the king respond when he discovers Mordecai's role in thwarting the assassination plot (vv. 2-6)?

---

3. Where do you see irony in King Xerxes' and Haman's actions on this particular night (vv. 1-6 and 5:14)?

4. God has been working quietly to bring together many of the incidents recorded in this chapter. He uses insignificant things to work out his plans. Describe a time where God used an insignificant thing in your life for his purposes.

5. What else can we discern about Haman's character through his response to the king's question in verses 7-9?

6. Pick either King Xerxes, Mordecai or Haman, and describe what that character would have been feeling during this eventful day.

7. Haman seeks comfort from his wife and friends after his ride through the city with Mordecai, but he receives a very different response. How do his wife and advisers interpret the situation and react to Haman (vv. 12-14)? Why?

8. How do they seem to be distancing themselves from Haman?

9. How has Haman's life been a picture of Jesus' words in Luke 14:11?

10. Think back to the group activity or the personal reflection. What are some negative consequences of the un-Christlike character trait you identified?

11. What is one step you can take this week to allow God's redemptive power to work in this area of your life?

Pray for the Holy Spirit's continual work in transforming your character.

Now or Later

Study Luke 14:1-24. Look for what Jesus says about pride and humility.

7

Character No Matter What

This is what the wicked are like—
   always carefree, they increase in wealth.
Surely in vain have I kept my heart pure;
   in vain have I washed my hands in innocence.
PSALM 73:12-13

These words express the struggle in the heart of the psalmist. He is wrestling because he does not see justice being carried out; instead, the wicked prosper and the righteous are plagued.

GROUP DISCUSSION. Justice is sometimes difficult to grasp and to see. The complexity of situations can make working toward justice arduous. In order to get a glimpse of the complexities in life, select a current world issue as a group. Discuss what justice would look like in this situation.

PERSONAL REFLECTION. In what area of your life or community do you long to see justice lived out?

Esther and Mordecai have chosen to do what is right throughout the story, yet they face destruction. Haman, who is prideful, angry and bitter, has been successful in plotting against the Jews. Finally, in chapter 7 Esther and Mordecai see justice taking place. We are called to consistent character whether or not justice prevails in this life. In this study we will see what happens when the hidden things are revealed. *Read Esther 7.*

---

1. Name all of the truths that were previously hidden but are now revealed in this chapter.

---

2. Pretend you are directing a movie of Esther and you are filming this scene. How would you set up this scene? What would be important for each actor/actress to portray?

---

3. How does Esther present her request (vv. 3-4)?

4. What thoughts and emotions might the king and Haman experience when Esther presents her request (vv. 6-7)?

5. What is ironic about the events of this banquet?

6. What do verses 6-8 reveal about Haman's character?

7. How do you see justice carried out in the lives of Esther, Mordecai and Haman?

8. How do justice and doing what is right work together?

What struggles do you face when these things do not seem to be working together?

---

9. How can you (individually or corporately) seek justice or do what is right in a situation where you currently see injustice?

---

10. How will you respond if justice is not served?

Pray for an area of injustice for which your heart breaks.

Now or Later

Commit to reading a book about the area of injustice you have identified. Pick a book that thoughtfully deals with the issues of justice and the complexity of life. You can read this individually or with a group.

8

Praising God's Faithfulness

As the sunshine filtered through the sanctuary windows, the pastor stood and asked for the congregation to share how God had been faithful. One by one the people rose to their feet. There were testimonies about marriages restored, physical healings, new passion for service, children coming to Christ and spiritual growth. I listened with a joyful heart; certainly God is faithful!

GROUP DISCUSSION. Gather around a large piece of blank paper. Have each person write down instances of God's faithfulness in their own lives or in the pages of Scripture as they come to mind. When the page is filled with the record of God's faithfulness, read through the notes on the paper, remembering and telling stories.

PERSONAL REFLECTION. Journal about a time when God has proven himself faithful to you in a difficult situation.

The book of Esther shows that sometimes justice comes in the way we expected, and at other times we are surprised by God's ways. But one thing remains certain: God is faithful. He will provide and care for his people. From overwhelming opposition to the smallest concern, God continues to be faithful to us. God provides not only for Esther and Mordecai but for all of his people. Because he has been faithful, the people respond with rejoicing and celebrating. Our response to God should be no different. *Read Esther 8.*

---

1. List all the ways that Esther and Mordecai are rewarded by God through the actions of the king.

---

2. In verses 3-6 we see a little more of Esther's character and heart. What do these verses reveal about her?

---

3. Esther felt deep concern and compassion for her people. For what person or group of people would you like to have that same kind of concern?

How might you develop compassion for them?

4. How does King Xerxes respond to Esther's plea (vv. 7-10)?

5. How did the edict that Mordecai issued (vv. 11-13) provide what Esther was asking for in verses 5-6 without breaking the first edict (3:12-14)?

6. How was this God's provision and protection for his people?

7. What is the response of the Jews to God's provision and protection (vv. 15-17)?

8. How did the response of the Jews to the first edict in chapter 4 (4:1-3, 15-16) pave the way for the events of this chapter?

---

9. How can we respond when we are waiting for God to act in our lives?

---

10. Think over the past week, and share how God has been faithful to you. What is one way you can express to God your joy and gladness about his provision for you?

Pray in gratitude for God's faithfulness to your group or to you personally, or pray for someone in the group who is still waiting for God to act.

Now or Later
Study Hebrews 11, the "faith chapter." Look for all the ways that God provided for his people. Wrestle with the second half of the chapter where it seems God did not provide or protect. How does this section fit into the passage and into our understanding of God's activity in our lives?

9

Remembering & Celebrating

It was a beautiful spring day, and I was walking along a dirt road that wound through the mountains outside Bear Trap Ranch in Colorado. I was pouring out my heart to God and wrestling with where he wanted to take me in my life. As I strolled among the pine trees, God opened my eyes to the abundant life that lay before me if I would commit my future to his service. That moment changed the course of my life, and I am eternally grateful to the Lord. Every time I visit Bear Trap Ranch I walk along that very road and remember that moment and God's faithfulness to me. Remembering helps me keep my perspective and empowers me to go on in my commitment to his service.

When God does something in our midst it is important to remember it and to celebrate. As we recollect his goodness, our faith is strengthened and so is our ability to face the next struggle.

GROUP DISCUSSION. Before this study ask each group member to bring something that represents an event or occasion that they commemorate. Have each person describe the item and how they and their family celebrate this particular occasion.

PERSONAL REFLECTION. What is something in your life or the life of your family that you wish you celebrated or that you wish you celebrated differently?

The last chapter of Esther causes internal conflict for many of us. The description of the destruction of life is unsettling, yet this was part of the experience of the chosen people. This passage is unique because the description of death is set in the context of celebration, not for the loss of life but for the faithfulness of God. *Read Esther 9—10.*

---

1. Summarize the events of the thirteenth, fourteenth and fifteenth days of Adar.

---

2. Describe the people who were actually destroyed by the Jews on these days (9:5-17).

3. The author mentions three separate times that the Jews did not lay their hands on their enemies' plunder. Why might the Jews have left the plunder despite the king's permission to take it (9:10, 15-16)?

4. What emotions and thoughts occur in you as you read this chapter?

5. Mordecai and Esther proclaimed and established the celebration of Purim as a holiday for all the Jews. What was the purpose of the celebration (9:20-27)?

6. The wording in 9:28 emphasizes the importance of the celebration for all the Jews. Why is the observation of Purim so crucial?

7. How were the Jews instructed to celebrate Purim (9:22)?

8. How is the celebration of Purim different from most of our celebrations?

---

9. God has saved his people and blessed Esther and Mordecai for their obedience to him. Summarize what happens to Esther and Mordecai at the end of the story (9:29—10:3).

---

10. What qualities did Mordecai have that made him a respected leader?

---

11. Throughout Scripture God instructs his people to commemorate the times when he acted to provide for and save his people. Why is remembering God's acts of faithfulness important for us as Christians?

---

12. What is one thing that God has done for you or for your group that you would truly like to remember?

What are some ways you could celebrate it (individually or as a group)?

Praise God for the things in your life worth celebrating.

Now or Later

Host a Purim celebration as a group (see the leader's notes for details).

Have a Jewish believer come to your group and talk with you about the book of Esther and Purim celebrations in his/her own life.

Read a book that discusses the issues of violence in the Old Testament.

Leader's Notes

MY GRACE IS SUFFICIENT FOR YOU. (2 COR 12:9)

Leading a Bible discussion can be an enjoyable and rewarding experience. But it can also be *scary*—especially if you've never done it before. If this is your feeling, you're in good company. When God asked Moses to lead the Israelites out of Egypt, he replied, "O Lord, please send someone else to do it"! (Ex 4:13). It was the same with Solomon, Jeremiah and Timothy, but God helped these people in spite of their weaknesses, and he will help you as well.

You don't need to be an expert on the Bible or a trained teacher to lead a Bible discussion. The idea behind these inductive studies is that the leader guides group members to discover for themselves what the Bible has to say. This method of learning will allow group members to remember much more of what is said than a lecture would.

These studies are designed to be led easily. As a matter of fact, the flow of questions through the passage from observation to interpretation to application is so natural that you may feel that the studies lead themselves. This study guide is also flexible. You can use it with a variety of groups—student, professional, neighborhood or church groups. Each study takes forty-five to sixty minutes in a group setting.

There are some important facts to know about group dynamics and encouraging discussion. The suggestions listed below should enable you to effectively and enjoyably fulfill your role as leader.

Preparing for the Study

1. Ask God to help you understand and apply the passage in your own life. Unless this happens, you will not be prepared to lead others. Pray too for the various members of the group. Ask God to open your hearts to the message of his Word and motivate you to action.

2. Read the introduction to the entire guide to get an overview of the entire book and the issues which will be explored.

3. As you begin each study, read and reread the assigned Bible passage to familiarize yourself with it.

4. This study guide is based on the New International Version of the Bible. It will help you and the group if you use this translation as the basis for your study and discussion.

5. Carefully work through each question in the study. Spend time in meditation and reflection as you consider how to respond.

6. Write your thoughts and responses in the space provided in the study guide. This will help you to express your understanding of the passage clearly.

7. It might help to have a Bible dictionary handy. Use it to look up any unfamiliar words, names or places. (For additional help on how to study a passage, see chapter five of *How to Lead a LifeBuilder Study*, IVP, 2018.)

8. Consider how you can apply the Scripture to your life. Remember that the group will follow your lead in responding to the studies. They will not go any deeper than you do.

9. Once you have finished your own study of the passage, familiarize yourself with the leader's notes for the study you are leading. These are designed to help you in several ways. First, they tell you the purpose the study guide author had in mind when writing the study. Take time to think through how the study questions work together to accomplish that purpose. Second, the notes provide you with additional background information or suggestions on group dynamics for various questions. This information can be useful when people have difficulty understanding or answering a question. Third, the leader's notes can alert you to potential problems you may encounter during the study.

10. If you wish to remind yourself of anything mentioned in the leader's notes, make a note to yourself below that question in the study.

Leading the Study

1. Begin the study on time. Open with prayer, asking God to help the group to understand and apply the passage.

2. Be sure that everyone in your group has a study guide. Encourage the group to prepare beforehand for each discussion by reading the introduction to the guide and by working through the questions in the study.

3. At the beginning of your first time together, explain that these studies are meant to be discussions, not lectures. Encourage the members of the group to participate. However, do not put pressure on those who may be hesitant to speak during the first few sessions. You may want to suggest the following guidelines to your group.

☐ Stick to the topic being discussed.

☐ Your responses should be based on the verses which are the focus of the discussion and not on outside authorities such as commentaries or speakers.

☐ These studies focus on a particular passage of Scripture. Only rarely should you refer to other portions of the Bible. This allows for everyone to participate in in-depth study on equal ground.

☐ Anything said in the group is considered confidential and will not be discussed outside the group unless specific permission is given to do so.

☐ We will listen attentively to each other and provide time for each person present to talk.

☐ We will pray for each other.

4. Have a group member read the introduction at the beginning of the discussion.

5. Every session begins with a group discussion question. The question or activity is meant to be used before the passage is read. The question introduces the theme of the study and encourages group members to begin to open up. Encourage as many members as possible to participate, and be ready to get the discussion going with your own response.

This section is designed to reveal where our thoughts or feelings need to be transformed by Scripture. That is why it is especially important not to read the passage before the discussion question is asked. The passage will tend to color the honest reactions people would otherwise give because they are, of course, supposed to think the way the Bible does.

You may want to supplement the group discussion question with an icebreaker to help people to get comfortable. See the community section of the *Small Group Starter Kit* (IVP, 1995) for more ideas.

You also might want to use the personal reflection question with your group. Either allow a time of silence for people to respond individually or discuss it together.

6. Have a group member (or members if the passage is long) read aloud the passage to be studied. Then give people several minutes to read the passage again silently so that they can take it all in.

7. Question 1 will generally be an overview question designed to briefly survey the passage. Encourage the group to look at the whole passage, but try to avoid getting sidetracked by questions or issues that will be addressed later in the study.

8. As you ask the questions, keep in mind that they are designed to be used just as they are written. You may simply read them aloud. Or you may prefer to express them in your own words.

There may be times when it is appropriate to deviate from the study guide. For example, a question may have already been answered. If so, move on to the next question. Or someone may raise an important question not covered in the guide. Take time to discuss it, but try to keep the group from going off on tangents.

9. Avoid answering your own questions. If necessary, repeat or rephrase them until they are clearly understood. Or point out something you read in the leader's notes to clarify the context or meaning. An eager group quickly becomes passive and silent if they think the leader will do most of the talking.

10. Don't be afraid of silence. People may need time to think about the question before formulating their answers.

11. Don't be content with just one answer. Ask, "What do the rest of you think?" or "Anything else?" until several people have given answers to the question.

12. Acknowledge all contributions. Try to be affirming whenever possible. Never reject an answer. If it is clearly off-base, ask, "Which verse led you to that conclusion?" or again, "What do the rest of you think?"

13. Don't expect every answer to be addressed to you, even though this will probably happen at first. As group members become more at ease, they will begin to truly interact with each other. This is one sign of healthy discussion.

14. Don't be afraid of controversy. It can be very stimulating. If you don't resolve an issue completely, don't be frustrated. Move on and keep it in mind for later. A subsequent study may solve the problem.

15. Periodically summarize what the group has said about the passage. This helps to draw together the various ideas mentioned and gives continuity to the study. But don't preach.

16. At the end of the Bible discussion you may want to allow group members a time of quiet to work on an idea under "Now or Later." Then discuss what you experienced. Or you may want to encourage group members to work on these ideas between meetings. Give an opportunity during the session for people to talk about what they are learning.

17. Conclude your time together with conversational prayer, adapting the prayer suggestion at the end of the study to your group. Ask for God's help in following through on the commitments you've made.

18. End on time.

Many more suggestions and helps are found in *How to Lead a LifeBuilder Study*.

Components of Small Groups

A healthy small group should do more than study the Bible. There are four components to consider as you structure your time together.

Nurture. Small groups help us to grow in our knowledge and love of God. Bible study is the key to making this happen and is the foundation of your small group.

Community. Small groups are a great place to develop deep friendships with other Christians. Allow time for informal interaction before and after each study. Plan activities and games that will help you get to know each other. Spend time having fun together—going on a picnic or cooking dinner together.

Worship and prayer. Your study will be enhanced by spending time praising God together in prayer or song. Pray for each other's needs—

and keep track of how God is answering prayer in your group. Ask God to help you to apply what you are learning in your study.

Outreach. Reaching out to others can be a practical way of applying what you are learning, and it will keep your group from becoming self-focused. Host a series of evangelistic discussions for your friends or neighbors. Clean up the yard of an elderly friend. Serve at a soup kitchen together, or spend a day working in the community.

Many more suggestions and helps in each of these areas are found in the *Small Group Starter Kit.* You will also find information on building a small group. Reading through the starter kit will be worth your time.

Study 1. Esther 1. A Little Respect.
Purpose: To show that respect between individuals is built through mutual regard and appreciation rather than demanding respect or controlling one another.
Group discussion. Every study begins with a group discussion question. They are helpful for a variety of reasons.

First, they help the group to warm up to each other. No matter how well a group may know each other, there is always a stiffness that needs to be overcome before people will begin to talk openly. A good question will break the ice.

Second, discussion questions get people thinking along the lines of the topic of the study. Most people will have lots of different things going on in their minds (dinner, an important meeting coming up, how to get the car fixed) that will have nothing to do with the study. A creative question will get their attention and draw them into the discussion.

Third, discussion questions can reveal where our thoughts or feelings need to be transformed by Scripture. That is why it is especially important not to read the passage before the approach question is asked. The passage will tend to color the honest reactions people would otherwise give because they are, of course, supposed to think the way the Bible does. Giving honest responses before they find out what the Bible says may help them see where their thoughts or attitudes need to be changed.

Personal reflection. Each study has a personal reflection question as well. These are designed for your use in personal devotions. This question will help open your mind to the topic of the study and begin to establish the connection between your own story and the story contained in the Scripture passage. Try not to skim over this question, but instead take a few minutes to carefully and honestly respond. This will help illuminate the areas of your own life that need transforming by the Holy Spirit.

Question 1. Try to enter the text with this question. Imagining yourself at a celebration like this might include observing the smells of curry, rice, wine, rich spices and oils. The air would most likely be filled with music, laughter and talking. Try to discuss what you might be feeling if you were there.

Question 2. The list and type of guests at King Xerxes' banquet give us a glimpse into the earthly power and prestige assembled.

Besides naming the main characters, such as King Xerxes and Queen Vashti, make sure the group names the nobles, officials, military leaders, princes, people from the citadel of Susa, the wives of these guests, eunuchs and wise men. Being aware of who was invited to the party will help the group in answering some of the other questions.

Question 3. The author spends several verses describing the details of this celebration—the furnishings, the guests, the decorations and the abundant wine. The length of the celebration is also important. King Xerxes may have wanted to display his great wealth and power to the nobles and officials he had invited. It is likely that he took this opportunity to present his intention to attack Greece and to plan the campaign with his military leaders. (King Xerxes carried out his plans against Greece in 481 B.C.) If this was the case, King Xerxes may have been trying to show his guests his authority and power in the kingdom and his credibility in preparation for his Greek campaigns. Everyone would certainly have been impressed by the king's wealth and power.

Make sure the group observes the description of the wine. The free-flowing wine and each guest's freedom to consume as much wine as desired sets the tone for the events later in the chapter. It is likely that many of the male guests were "in high spirits" from the wine. King Xerxes is described that way as well. This probably influenced his later actions.

Question 4. It is important to the development of the study to spend some time discussing why King Xerxes made such a request of the queen. Help the group see how the scene has been set by the celebration. Note how the wine and the party may have led to such a request. The king has displayed all of his wealth and possessions and now desires to display his most beautiful treasure. His motive seems to have been to impress his guests further by showing off his wife's beauty. The motivation for the request seems tied to his desire for the praise of people.

Question 5. There are several aspects to Vashti's predicament. The request is not a noble one. The king wants her to appear in front of his drunken guests only to display herself. To obey the request would mean degrading herself in front of the guests. At the same time, refusing to obey the king's command would most certainly bring about serious consequences. Her disobedience, especially in front of the people the king was trying to impress, would place Xerxes in an awkward position as well; his authority would be questioned. It is unlikely that Vashti would have refused the king without careful thought. She must have felt strongly enough about the situation to risk the consequences for disobedience.

Vashti's decision is an important element in the book. Because of Vashti's refusal, there will be a search for a new queen, which allows Esther to enter the story and save her people. Help the group place themselves in Vashti's position and wrestle with the decision she faces.

Question 6. Even though we have only a few verses so far on which to base speculation about the king's character, it is possible to make some initial comments. Because of his extravagance and the nature of his request to Vashti, King Xerxes seems to be a man caught up in his own wealth and power. He appears to be a prideful man whose worth rests in praise and recognition from others and in his possessions. Further, in his request of the queen, King Xerxes shows that he doesn't respect Queen Vashti as a person.

Question 9. Respect for authority is healthy and necessary, but the process of gaining that respect is viewed differently by the characters. King Xerxes uses wealth and power to try and impress others as a means of gaining respect. The wise men think respect is something that must be demanded and gained through forced obedience, not mutual respect and appreciation. Vashti is willing to take a stand on something she feels strongly about, which is a respectful choice.

Question 10. If respect develops between people, it is because there is mutual regard and appreciation. The dictionary tells us that respect involves showing esteem, consideration and honor for the other person. This is the point where you can direct the group back to their answers to the first question. Discussing why they respect someone should help them determine how respect is gained.

Study 2. Esther 2. Trusting God's Work.

Purpose: To recognize God's ordering work in our lives and to learn to trust his direction.

Group discussion and personal reflection. It is helpful to identify how God has brought circumstances together in our lives. He fits experiences together to prepare us for his work and to transform our characters. Try to see how you have been prepared or transformed.

Question 1. Note that four years have passed since Queen Vashti was dethroned. Compare 2:16, which cites the seventh year of King Xerxes' reign, and 1:2, which takes place in the third year of King Xerxes' reign. During the time between Vashti's disposal and the events in chapter 2, King Xerxes was occupied with his military campaigns in Greece. It was after his defeat in 479 B.C. that he returned to Susa and remembered what had happened to Vashti.

Question 3. Imagine Mordecai's anxiety over the future of his cousin Esther. He would probably have been sad to have Esther taken from his care and worried about her treatment. He might also have been hopeful about her possibly holding such an honored position with the chance to have an influence on the kingdom.

Esther might have also had a range of emotions during the lengthy process, including excitement, hope, fear, sadness and uncertainty.

Question 4. Esther won favor with Hegai, the king and all those who saw her; she was indeed beautiful. However, it seems that Esther would not have won everyone's approval if she possessed only physical beauty. Esther's presence, demeanor and personality must have been part of her appeal. Verse 17 implies the king found her appealing not just in the physical sense.

Each woman who was ready to appear before the king was offered anything she wanted to take with her. She could have requested jewels, clothing, cosmetics or other ornaments to enhance her beauty and her chance of being chosen. Esther chose only those things that Hegai suggested. Certainly her humility and modesty would have shown.

In studying character throughout this book you'll find that a person's character and presence affects others and is appealing—or repelling. How people view us says a lot about our character.

Question 6. The purpose of these women and the harem in general was to provide pleasure for the king. They had no rights, and their lives were restricted and probably very dull. They remained in the harem until the king called them by name (v. 12). If they were called, they would go to the king to give him sexual pleasure. The women who were not crowned queen would most likely live out their lives much like widows (v. 14). If Esther had not been chosen, she would have become one of those women forgotten by the king.

This concept will appear again in question 10 as one of the circumstances God orchestrates to accomplish his plans. Because Esther was the queen, she had more rights, freedom, influence and authority than the other women; she was in a position where she could accomplish more for God when the time came.

Question 7. Mordecai might have been uncertain as to how Esther would be treated if her identity was known. He may also have had some sense of God's hand in the process of her becoming queen. Perhaps he felt that there would be an appropriate time for disclosure.

Question 9. We have not seen a tremendous amount of Mordecai yet in the story, but just as the plot of a movie unfolds scene after scene, more and more about a person's character can be observed with each glimpse into that person's life. Mordecai displays integrity in his choice to reveal the assassination plot against the king even though there may have been risks involved. Mordecai also shows deep concern for Esther by continuing to seek out information about her. He does not leave her in the palace and forget about her but instead goes to visit each day.

People put together a picture of our character from the times they interact with us, no matter how briefly. God wants us to be people of godly, consistent character, and that means choosing to do what is right in all situations.

Question 10. Guide the group in looking at the many ways God has been at work to set things in place: Esther's being blessed with extraordinary beauty; Mordecai's being employed at the king's gate so that he hears the assassination plot; Queen Vashti's refusal in the first chapter, which leads to the search for a new queen; God's working in the hearts and minds of those Esther encounters so that she wins their approval; and Mordecai's name and deed being recorded in the annals of the king. The group will begin to see how God is orchestrating events and circumstances so that everything will be in place when the threat from Haman surfaces. As you work through the study guide, help the group to see how God does this throughout the whole book.

Now or later. This can be a fascinating study to do in the life of another biblical character. Moses was prepared to shepherd the people of God and to be the spokesman for the Hebrews in the Egyptian court. His life is full of God's handiwork in preparing him for his role.

Study 3. Esther 3. Evaluating Advice.

Purpose: To discover how to evaluate the counsel we receive from others and to give good advice.

Group discussion. The list should include items such as television, newspapers, magazines, family and neighbors. This will broaden the list and give people the opportunity to see pros and cons in each one. For instance, magazines may alert you to something you are not aware of, but the values on which the perspective is based may not be kingdom values.

Question 2. The conflict between Mordecai and Haman begins with Mordecai's refusing to honor Haman by bowing down to him.

Although this initiates the conflict, the history between Mordecai's people, the Jews, and Haman's people, the Amalekites, intensifies the problem. The Jewish people bowed before kings and other people at times throughout their history to show honor and respect (Gen 33:3; 1 Sam 24:8; 1 Kings 1:16). So the reason Mordecai refuses to honor Haman in this way is probably not because he felt he would be worshiping Haman as a god. The reason stems from the intense rivalry between the Amalekites and the Jews.

It will be necessary to review the story of the conflict before moving on in the study. The leader can summarize the story, or the group may look up the relevant passages and read about the history themselves. Knowing the story is important, because Haman's intense response to Mordecai is a result of the long-standing conflict between their peoples. This will help the group understand Haman and Mordecai much better. The Scriptures to which you can direct the group are Exodus 17:8-16, Deuteronomy 25:17-19 and 1 Samuel 15:1-33.

Question 4. Verses 8-9 are fascinating. Help the group to look closely at the way Haman approaches the subject, how he manipulates the king and appeals to Xerxes' greed and desire for power. For example, Haman knows that his offer of money will appeal to the king. He also knows that the king will not like the idea that there are people in his kingdom who challenge his authority by not obeying his rule. The Jews did in fact have their own customs, but they were obedient to the king and did not cause any trouble in the kingdom. Furthermore, Haman is careful not to reveal the name of the people he wants destroyed or that his motivation for their destruction comes from his own personal anger. In fact, Haman comes across as a concerned subject wishing to protect the king and to act in the king's best interest. Haman weaves a tapestry of truth, half-truths and lies in order to convince the king of his plan.

There is historical evidence that monarchs at times violently repressed uprisings and potential threats in their kingdoms. King Xerxes' decision to destroy this supposedly threatening people group would not necessarily have been entirely abnormal.

Question 5. It will be easy for the group to see Haman's manipulation and deceit in this chapter. However, this question will give them a chance to see how easily we can act in the same ways. Guide the group in relating experiences where it was tempting for them to try to manipulate another for their gain or to stretch the truth so they appeared to be doing the right thing. If details feel too personal, then focus on the thoughts and feelings in the midst of the situation. We are frequently guilty of the very same things as Haman.

Question 6. The detailed description shows how extensive and well functioning the postal and communication systems of the kingdom were. So it was feasible for the entire kingdom to follow through on the edict and annihilate all of the Jews in the kingdom.

Question 7. The author uses repetition of words such as *each, every* and *all* to emphasize the intensity of the threat against the Jews. The author also spends several verses describing how and where the edict was issued. The detail and repetition set the scene for the reader. The edict would touch the life of every Jew; no one would be missed. The threat against them was overwhelming and all-encompassing.

Question 9. King Xerxes shows more of his character by the way he is so easily convinced to destroy a whole group of people by an appeal to his greed and pride. Several commentators believe that the king did accept the money Haman offered and that the refusal was merely politeness and custom. The last verse of this chapter reveals even more about Xerxes. He and Haman sit down to drink, totally unconcerned about the people whose destruction they have ordered. He shows a lack of concern or compassion.

Question 11. You may want to refer back to the introduction and the quote from Tozer. Help the group think through the ways that we give unwise advice and how we can keep ourselves from falling into those patterns. It is crucial that before we offer counsel we are willing to seek the Lord for his wisdom and insight about the situation, and also that we are willing to hear the Lord speak about things in our own lives. We must remain humble before God and others when giving advice.

Question 12. Be sure to allow enough time for a good discussion of this question. It is easy for us to be swayed by others and to act on the counsel of others even when the advice is poor. Seeking the Lord's wisdom, speaking to several people, comparing the advice with Scripture and being selective with the people you choose to seek counsel from are several ways you can evaluate advice. Help the group wrestle with the necessity to evaluate any counsel they receive.

Study 4. Esther 4. Doing the Right Thing.
Purpose: To recognize the situations in which God has placed you to do his will, and to commit to acting with courage and integrity in those situations.

Group discussion. Come prepared for your group with newspapers or magazines. The goal is to find stories that describe the tough situations in which people find themselves and the difficult decisions they face. We want to help people see that even in everyday life we have the choice of doing what is right or wrong and facing the consequences before God.

Question 2. Mordecai responded to the news about the edict by tearing his clothes, putting on sackcloth and ashes, and mourning. He was grieving in every way possible. He was publicly displaying his grief about the situation by wailing through the city streets.

The Jews responded in the same ways as Mordecai. There was great mourning, fasting, weeping and wailing. It is important to note that in every place the edict went there was the same reaction. This is a strong example of community and the connectedness of the Jews as a people.

The Jews wore sackcloth and ashes when mourning in hopes of averting national catastrophe. Help the group see that the Jews immediately turned to their God for help; they sought God's protection and mercy before doing anything else. This sometimes is not our first response to tragic news.

Question 3. There has been great feasting and celebrating in the book so far (1:3-9; 2:18; 3:15). Haman and the king sit down for a drink, which seems to be a joyful, relaxed situation. Help the group see the contrast between the feasting of Haman and the king, and the mourning of the Jewish people. It seems that these two men have determined the fate of a whole people, but in reality the fate of the Jews remains with the sovereign God.

Questions 4-5. Esther first responds to Mordecai's display of mourning with, perhaps, embarrassment because she is unaware of the plot against the Jews. Once she is informed of the plot and of Mordecai's request, her emotions and response quickly change.

Esther first reacts by thinking about the risks she personally faces in going to the king. If a person approaches the king without being summoned, that person is in danger of being put to death unless the king gives a pardon. At this point Esther is not thinking about helping her people or using her position to influence the fate of the Jews. She is probably afraid, nervous and uncertain when she receives Mordecai's first message.

Her final response is to realize the truth of Mordecai's words and resign herself to the path in front of her. She knows that she must approach the king and that her fate is in his hands. But she realizes that her obedience to God must come first. She is experiencing great determination and resignation here, even in the midst of her fear.

Knowing that Esther thinks about her own safety first is helpful because it highlights her final decision to carry out Mordecai's instructions. The fact that she was afraid but had the courage and character to go through with it anyway is motivating.

Question 7. Mordecai is aware of the influential position Esther holds as the queen. He realizes the potential she has in affecting this situation. He also knows that God has placed her in this position for a reason, and he reveals that to Esther in verse 14. Mordecai pleads with Esther because she is the only one who has access to the king.

Question 8. Mordecai's arguments highlight some very important principles for Esther. He reminds her that there are consequences for failing to do what God asks. If Esther refuses to help her people, she will be a victim of Haman's plot as well. Mordecai also persuades her by helping her see the divine intervention in her becoming the queen so that she would be in a position to help her people when the time came. Divine intervention is a very important concept for the group to touch on because it reminds us that God does place us in relationships, jobs or locations for a reason.

Question 9. The themes of the book of Esther are seen most clearly in this chapter. The relationship between God's sovereign work in the world and the response of his people is witnessed in Mordecai's arguments. Mordecai is convinced that God will still provide deliverance for the Jews even if Esther refuses to go to the king. God will not abandon his chosen people by letting them be completely destroyed. This is God's sovereignty. He is ultimately in control, and he will accomplish his plans.

However, God chooses to work through his people. If Esther decides to go to the king and plead for her people, she will be used by God and will experience the privilege of being part of the plan. If she chooses not to help, she will not keep God's plan from happening; she will only experience consequences for her inaction and miss out on the opportunity God gave her.

Again, it is important to help the group touch on this relationship. As they think through this in the context of Esther's situation, hopefully they will realize that God will accomplish his plans in their lives but that they do have a choice to be involved or to experience the consequences.

Question 10. The key character qualities that Esther shows are courage, dependence on God and moral strength. This is a good time to touch on verse 16, which shows that Esther turned to her people for support and that she knew she must turn to God in order to be able to face the risks.

Now or later. This would be a great group activity that takes the discussion further but gives the group a break from the regular study. Try to find a movie that has the theme of doing the right thing, and discuss the traits of each character—whether they choose what is right or not.

Study 5. Esther 5. The Heart of the Matter.

Purpose: To guard against facing difficult times or tasks with anger or bitterness, and to learn to face them with humility and dependence on God.

Question 1. Esther not only risks going before the king but delays answering him twice. She appears before him unsummoned, which could bring about her immediate death if the king does not extend a pardon. Esther does not know how the king will respond to her or her delays in stating her request. Esther also risks the plight of her people if she dies. Who will help them if she cannot?

Question 2. Try to encourage the group to really participate in this activity. Role-playing can make people hesitant, but it can help them see the characters in new ways. If it would help, feel free to come up with some questions together to ask Esther and then role-play. Try to get at Esther's feelings. Help the group discuss the fears Esther may have felt as well as the confidence from the support of God's people. Try to encourage the group to be as creative and thoughtful as possible.

Question 4. Chapter 3 talks about the fasting that Esther requested of her people and the fact that she fasted as well. Prayer usually accompanies such fasting. It seems consistent that her people were spending time fasting and interceding for her. Esther was no doubt deep in prayer at this point also. The prayers and fasting gave Esther strength and courage to carry out her plan. The recognition that God may have placed her in the position of queen for this specific purpose might have spurred her on as well.

Help the group talk about the ways Esther was strengthened and empowered so they will be reminded that we all desperately need the prayers and support of our friends and family in order to fulfill God's call and develop consistent character.

Question 5. The reason Esther makes this request is not specifically stated, but it is probable that in her times of fasting and prayer she felt God was instructing her to wait and approach the king in this way. Asking for two separate banquets also might have conveyed to the king the importance of her request. The delay in stating the request allowed for other events to surface, such as Haman's gallows and Mordecai's involvement in uncovering the assassination plot. Another motivation for Esther may have been the atmosphere of the court in comparison to the atmosphere of a banquet. There were no doubt many attendants and others in the court, and there would have been fewer people at a banquet for just the king and Haman. She may have felt it more appropriate to plead for her life and for her people in the banquet setting. It is important for the group to see that the Jews and Esther prayed and fasted before she made her careful plans. Too often we take action without seeking the Lord or the advice and support of our Christian community.

Question 6. Haman was an arrogant man who measured his worth by his power and influence over others. His goal was to control others and receive honor. He was controlled by anger, bitterness and pride.

Question 7. You can have the group members pair up and spend a few minutes in a mock interview again.

Make sure to address Haman's obsession with Mordecai. Haman was consumed with a racial hatred for the Jews, but his personal hatred for Mordecai stemmed from Mordecai's refusal to honor him. Mordecai's refusal challenged Haman's power and his self-centeredness. The things Haman boasted about held no joy for him because of the one thing he hated desperately—Mordecai. Hatred and bitterness in our lives will produce the same effects. Bitterness will sour everything and return again and again until we deal with it.

Question 8. The issue of doing what is right stands out in this question. Esther had courage and humility, and acted in the way that was right. She risked everything for God and her people, and Haman acted only for evil and self-interest

Now or later. This may be a very enlightening exercise but it may also be scary and unsettling. Make sure you have some friends to support you in the discovery process and in responding to what is revealed.

Study 6. Esther 6. Recognizing Unrighteousness.

Purpose: To identify those areas of our character that are displeasing to God and to present them before him, asking him to rid us of those traits.

Group discussion. This may be a difficult exercise for people to engage in, but encourage them to be creative. The idea is to have people identify an area of their life that needs transforming and then to get at how they feel about that or how they perceive that character trait by giving them another way of describing it. They can draw, create, write—whatever helps them articulate the thoughts and emotions associated with the question better. Have fun with this one!

Question 1. The book of Esther is full of examples of God working through circumstances to bring about his purposes. This chapter has plenty of seemingly coincidental incidents that again show us that God is in control and is working everything out for his good. The king happens to have trouble sleeping that night and happens to read the exact section of the book of the annals which recorded Mordecai's good deed. At the same time, Haman happens to be in the court when the king decides to honor Mordecai, and he ends up being the one who must honor Mordecai. God uses insignificant things to his glory and for his plans. This is a major theme in the book and is seen very clearly in this chapter.

Question 3. The construction of this book is incredible. The author uses repetition, irony, contrast and humor to communicate the story. It will be helpful to the group if they can see some of the irony contained in the story. On this particular night the king is preoccupied with how to honor someone who has done a good deed and has gone without recognition for five years. His intentions on this night are to honor; Haman's intentions are to destroy. He has also spent the night awake; however, he has occupied himself by building gallows on which to execute Mordecai. It is ironic that the very person both men are thinking about is Mordecai. Adding to the irony is the fact that Haman enters the court to approach the king about executing Mordecai, but he has no idea that he will leave the court to honor his adversary in front of the whole city.

Question 5. At this point have the group summarize the things they have already seen in Haman's character. The observations made in response to this question will add to the portrait. Help the group look through these three verses and discuss the motivations for suggesting such a reward.

Haman was already wealthy, but he desired popularity and recognition. He was obsessed with prestige. Haman did not suggest giving the honored man money or jewels, because he craved public acclaim. Again Haman's pride and arrogance are revealed.

Question 6. Xerxes would have had ongoing questions about what was happeing and who he should trust. He would have felt appreciative at some points, fearful at others.

Mordecai, on the other hand, might have started the day possibly praying for the Jews' situation, or for Esther. He might have been thinking and worrying about what was happening and the progress Esther was making. Yet at the end of the day he might have been overwhelmed with gratitude at the king's honoring him.

Haman would have gone through the whole range of emotions from accomplishment, joy and feelings of upcoming vindication to pride and pleasure at the thought of being honored by the king. He then would have moved into extreme humiliation, defeat, anger and bitterness.

Question 7. The response of Haman's wife and friends provides some interesting insight. First, Zeresh affirms Haman's downfall. Perhaps she realizes the power of the God of the Jews, or she recognizes the perseverance of the people through so much. Perhaps she is acknowledging the ultimate victory of the Jews over the Amalekites. Whatever the reason, she provides a gloomy picture.

Question 8. Haman's wife and friends in essence abandon him. They initially suggest building the gallows but now leave all the responsibility in the hands of Haman; he is alone in his suffering. Even their language indicates their abandonment of him: they say *you* or *your* three times in one sentence. They are assuming no part in his humiliation or downfall.

Question 9. This is an important question for the group to discuss because it leads into the application questions. Haman's pride and desire for recognition worked against him to place him in a humiliating situation. The people in Susa would have known about the rivalry between Mordecai and Haman because of Mordecai's refusal to bow down to him at the king's gate. In this way Haman suffered the consequences of unrighteousness in his life. We too fall prey to our unrighteousness. We can be prideful, hateful, impatient, unloving and so on. And there are many times when we act according to our sin nature. We then suffer the consequences, whether they be broken relationships, physical tragedy or unrest in our hearts.

Study 7. Esther 7. Character No Matter What.
Purpose: To commit to doing what is right whether or not we experience justice in this life.
Group discussion. This is a tricky question because the aim is to dis-

cover all the variables involved in a world issue or a social concern. To ask the question "What is justice here?" is to look at the issue from the perspective of all parties involved. Try to get at the various implications and variables without derailing the whole study. Spend some time on this question, but move along into the study.

Question 1. This is the point in the story where everything comes out into the open. The truth is no longer hidden but is laid out for all to see and experience. Esther's nationality is revealed to the king and to Haman. King Xerxes finds out the identity of the people group Haman has coerced him into destroying. Esther and Xerxes discover that Haman has built a gallows for Mordecai's execution, and Haman's true character is most clearly revealed to the king. The scene depicts what Jesus talks about in John 3—those whose deeds are evil love darkness. Haman has kept a lot of things secret, but when they are brought into the light they cause his downfall.

This chapter is a good reminder to us that our evil deeds will come to light in the end—oftentimes in this life—and we will face the consequences of those deeds.

Question 2. Try to help the group get into each character's shoes. Esther knows the king will ask about her request, and she will have to ask for his mercy. She will be revealing her nationality with no idea of how the news will be received. She also does not know if the king will do anything to spare her people. She may be feeling nervous and anxious about the outcome of the evening. Haman is obsessed with Mordecai and is consumed with anger toward him. He has also just been through a humiliating experience in front of the whole city. He is probably fuming and embarrassed.

The king, on the other hand, has no knowledge of either Esther's situation or Haman's anger. He perhaps is curious to know Esther's request; he is enjoying himself at the banquet and relaxing over wine.

Question 3. There is a great deal contained in these two verses. Guide the group through each part of Esther's request so they will be able to see how she handles herself before the king. This gives some more insight into her character as well. Esther begins her request with politeness and courtesy. She asks the king if she has found favor. She states her request very plainly, perhaps indicating her desperation. Her first request would have revealed her identity and taken Xerxes by surprise, but she quickly proceeds to plead for her people, not just herself. She describes the threat against her people by using the exact words of the edict.

There is some question about the meaning of her statement in verse 4. The group might wrestle with how Esther could have thought being sold into slavery was not worthy of bothering the king. However, there are two ways of looking at her comment. One is that she was making reference to the king's financial concerns and that the destruction of the Jews would be a loss to him. The other possibility is that she felt that to bother the king with a request was a serious undertaking, and the selling of her people would not have been serious enough to bother him.

Question 4. Many of their thoughts and emotions may come up in the answers to other questions, but it is good to have the group again put themselves into the shoes of the characters. It will help them interact with the passage more deeply.

King Xerxes is surprised at the nationality of his wife and horrified that he has played a part in plotting against her people. His official seal finalized the edict that ordered their destruction. He is extremely angry with Haman for manipulating him and coercing him into this situation.

His reaction is to leave for the garden, taking time to decide on the punishment or to cool down enough to even speak. Haman is terrified because everything has been reversed for him in a matter of minutes. He has discovered that his plan threatened the life of the queen, and he realizes his life is now in danger.

Question 5. Noting the irony allows the group to see how masterfully the author communicates the story. It is ironic that Haman is uncovered by a Jew, one of his enemies. It is ironic that he must beg Esther, a Jew, for his life, and that his life comes to an end on the very gallows that he built to end the life of his adversary. Haman believed he would be honored, and now he faces death. Esther believed she might die, but now she will be honored.

Question 6. Haman's response is to beg the queen for mercy. In so doing he breaks a strict rule of court etiquette. To approach the queen and speak to her without the king present was to cause great offense. He risks it in order to try one last plea for his life. His timing is horrible, and his fate is sealed.

The group might have difficulty delving this deeply into the reactions of Xerxes and Haman, so keep reminding them of all the truths that have now come out, and ask them how each man would have reacted to each revelation.

Question 8. This is a key question because it brings together the passage and our experience in life. We see in the passage justice being carried out. The wicked are punished, but the righteous are rewarded. Those who have integrity and godly character triumph. But in our experience this is not always what happens. We choose to do what is right but are not rewarded; sometimes our situations become worse because of our right choices. Our motivation for doing what is right is in understanding that justice will ultimately occur. We may not witness justice in this life, but we know from Scripture that justice will be done. Psalm 73 reminds us that when we are frustrated with the lack of justice, we must go to the sanctuary of God for his perspective. We must continue to do what is right whether or not justice happens now.

Study 8. Esther 8. Praising God's Faithfulness.

Purpose. To be aware of God's faithfulness in our lives and to continually praise him for it.

Group discussion. You will need to come prepared with a large piece of paper; a roll of newsprint works the best. Be sure to bring markers as well. The goal is to create a simultaneous recording of God's work in our lives and in the lives of people throughout history. Reading the stories can create an atmosphere of remembrance and gratitude. Playing music while you are doing the exercise can help to set the tone as well.

Question 1. This is an overview question that helps the group see how God provided for Mordecai and Esther. King Xerxes awards the estate of Haman to Esther. The estate of a person, that is, everything that a person owned, was reverted to the throne when that person became a condemned criminal. So all of Haman's belongings become Xerxes', which he then presents to Esther as compensation for the plot against her people. Mordecai is first of all brought into the court, then given the position of manager of Haman's estate. He is given Xerxes' signet ring, which would signify his legal authority to act in the king's name. Look throughout the whole chapter, because even in the last few verses we see more of Mordecai's rewards. In verse 15 we see Mordecai dressed in royal colors and royal robes, which demonstrate his position as second only to the king himself.

This is a good place to discuss the relationship between doing what is right and receiving rewards on earth. In the book of Esther, Mordecai and Esther faithfully serve God and do what is right, and they receive earthly rewards. However, we must be careful not to let earthly rewards be our motivation for choosing to do what is right. They may come or they may not. God does not promise that we will receive rewards here on earth for our service to him. Our motivation should be our love for God and for others and our desire to be Christlike.

Question 2. Esther is still grieving even though she has received many rewards. She has not forgotten the plight of her people. The horrible plot against the Jews is still in motion, and so she must go to the king once more. She expresses her deep love, compassion and concern for her people through her weeping, begging and pleading before the king. She is connected with them; they are her own people. Her heart will not rest until there is relief for them.

Esther shows her true character in these few verses. She shows that she is not self-seeking. Her motivation for approaching the king initially is not out of concern for her own well-being; her heart is for her people.

We fail so frequently in feeling compassion deeply for those around us. We are so often seeking our own comfort and security that we miss the suffering of others. Do we feel so connected with other people or other Christians that we seek out ways of relieving their plight? Would we risk our security, our lives for them?

Question 4. First, King Xerxes reminds Esther and Mordecai of what he has done for them already. But he does not stop at just rewarding them. He agrees to put a stop to the edict Haman instigated. He agrees to grant Esther's plea. However, the first edict can not be repealed. Once an edict was issued it could not be altered or revoked. The only way left for him to thwart the first edict is to allow a second one that will in some way minimize or offset the effects of the first. King Xerxes gives Mordecai the permission and authority to issue a second edict as he sees fit. The king puts at Mordecai's disposal the translators and secretaries of the court to work on the edict as well as the fastest horses in the kingdom to carry the edict as quickly as possible.

Questions 5-6. Mordecai attempted to construct an edict that would offset the effects of the initial order. The initial edict allowed the enemies of the Jews to destroy, kill and annihilate them on one particular day. So Mordecai issued an edict that allowed the Jews to gather together and protect themselves against this attack. They could kill those who sought to destroy them and plunder their property. Commentators differ on their opinions about this edict. Some say that the Jews were encouraged to seek revenge and attack any of their enemies without boundaries. Others hold the view that the Jews were instructed only to defend themselves and their families. Thus, any killing that would occur would be in self-defense and not all-out revenge. This explanation seems likely, and the NIV translation seems to indicate this in verse 11. It also appears unlikely that the king would have allowed an edict that would let the Jews attack the Persian people so overwhelmingly.

It is also important to help the group focus on how the second edict would offset the first and how God provides a way out for his people. Keep the focus on the Lord and his provision—the fact that the Jews faced incredible opposition, and yet God protected and saved them. His faithfulness is paramount. He is faithful not only to Esther and Mordecai, who served him so obediently, but to all his people.

Question 8. Chapter 4 describes how the Jews responded to the first edict. There was great mourning, fasting and weeping. The Jews immediately turned to their God for his mercy and protection. They knew that their only hope was in God, so they prayed. In this chapter we see the results of God's acting to provide for them. Now they are filled with joy. There is great contrast in the responses, but they are connected. The Jews first turned to God. He answered their prayers, and they responded to his faithfulness with feasting and celebrating.

This should lead nicely into the application questions about our own responses to God when he cares for us.

Study 9. Esther 9—10. Remembering & Celebrating.

Purpose: To learn to become people of thanksgiving, celebrating in tangible, glorifying ways the times when God has provided for us.

Group discussion. Try to prepare your group for this exercise the week before. Tell them you want them to bring something memorable that depicts a celebration in their home or in their family. This is similar to show-and-tell but with a deeper goal of building community in your group. A phone call to your group members is worth it. During the exercise encourage group members to ask questions of each other and to join in the spirit of celebration with each other.

Question 2. It is important to have the group look at what actually occurred during the days of destruction. As you read these last chapters of Esther, you may be struck by what seems to be a great slaughter of people by the Jews. They appear to show little mercy to their enemies. Helping the group focus on the text in answering this question will give some insight into the mindset of the Jews and into their motives.

The Jews acted in self-defense, attacking those who sought their destruction. There were boundaries to their actions. According to the text, they apparently attacked only their enemies. Question 3 adds further insight into their boundaries. It may be helpful to discuss verse 5 because the wording is somewhat difficult. It seems to imply that the Jews, following their human nature, did just what they wanted with their enemies, which is not a positive implication. However, the verse probably suggests that the Jews were free from any intervention on the part of the king's officials. This scene can be difficult for us to understand and may only truly be understood by those who have faced such persecution.

Question 3. Because the author mentions this three times, he obviously is trying to make a point. Several times in the history of the Jews the issue of taking their enemies' plunder surfaces. In Genesis 14:21-24 Abraham refuses the plunder from Sodom. Then later we witness Saul's descent from the favor of God because he takes plunder from his battle with the Amalekites. The Jewish people remembered this incident, and they refused to take the spoil even with King Xerxes' permission.

Ask the group what the Jews' refusing the plunder tells us about their motives in destroying their enemies. The Jews were not motivated by selfish gain or by enriching themselves personally with their enemies' property. They were not bent on a bloody revenge.

Question 4. This question is designed to help people articulate unsettling emotions about the killing of so many people. It may touch on people's difficulty in understanding many passages in the Old Testament where God commands his people to engage in the destruction of others. Help the group to wrestle with these questions and emotions as an honest part of the process of understanding God's actions in the world. Try to avoid simplistic or pat answers.

Question 6. The repetition of the word *every* emphasizes the importance of the Purim celebration to the Jews. It was something that everyone was to remember for all generations. It was viewed as a crucial time of remembrance because of the great saving act of God. The Jews as a people were saved from utter destruction. Their mourning was turned into joy by the goodness of God. Remembering would help them keep their perspective as to God's work in their lives as a people and would strengthen them in the face of other trials. Their celebration would be a rich fragrance to the Lord.

Questions 7-8. The Jews were instructed to celebrate by feasting and giving presents to each other and to the poor. By giving gifts to one another they emphasized the connectedness of the Jewish community, which experienced God's deliverance from Haman's plot. The gifts given to the poor were probably gifts of food so that those who were without the means to feast during Purim would be able to share the celebration. What a wonderful expression of community! The celebration of Purim helped to unite the people and encourage the whole community.

Direct the group in thinking through our own celebrations. Do we bring together the community, whether that be the body of Christ or families or small groups, through our celebrations? Do we focus on ourselves rather than recognizing those who are less fortunate? Are our celebrations of God's faithfulness glorifying to him, and do they help us to remember his mighty acts?

Questions 9-10. We can now put together some final observations about character. Esther is still concerned for her people. She is very active in the job of encouraging her people in the festival of Purim. She sees the value of the celebration and the benefits to the Jews. Mordecai remains unaffected by his place of power and prestige. In his position the temptation to become corrupt or work for personal gain may have been strong. Yet he strives for the good of the Jews, he speaks in their defense and for their welfare, and he is well received by the kingdom. This shows his strength of character and his high commitment to be a man of godly character.

Questions 11-12. If we desire to be people of godly character, we must recognize our need to remember and celebrate God's mighty acts. This glorifies the Lord and is a witness to those around us. Many times the apostle Paul exhorts us to be thankful. We worship the Lord when our lives are characterized by giving thanks for who God is and for what he has done in our midst.

The concept of planning some kind of remembrance or celebration for a particular incident where God provided may be a new concept for many, yet it would bring us together as a community of believers, enhance our thankfulness and be a testimony to the world, especially if we included others in some way. Help the group to be specific in their answers. This might be an opportunity for the group as a whole to plan something to celebrate what God has done in the group. Commemorating your experience together with the Lord would be a fitting way to end your study of Esther. Some other ideas for concluding the Esther study with a group are in the "Now or Later" section.

Now or later. The Jewish people still celebrate Purim today. One way to end the study may be to plan a traditional Purim celebration. Some of the things that are part of the celebration include feasting, hosting a costume ball where each person dresses as one of the characters from the book of Esther, and reading the book aloud while the party-goers cheer when Esther and Mordecai are mentioned and boo when Haman and others are mentioned. It is very much like a melodrama with audience participation.

Plan a celebration where the group distributes gifts to each other and to those who are less fortunate. This is also a way that we can celebrate God's faithfulness to us and be a witness to those around us by providing for them.

Patty Pell is a staff worker with InterVarsity Christian Fellowship on the campus of the University of Northern Colorado and at Christ Community Church in Greeley, Colorado. She is also the author of Hospitality *in the LifeBuilder Bible Study series.*

Printed and bound by CPI Group (UK) Ltd, Croydon, CR0 4YY

25/03/2025

14647345-0002